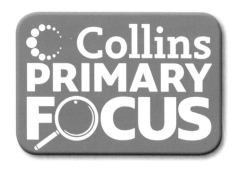

Spelling

Pupil Book 3

Joyce Vallar and Carol Doncaster

William Collins' dream of knowledge for all began with the publication of his first book in 1819. A self-educated mill worker, he not only enriched millions of lives, but also founded a flourishing publishing house. Today, staying true to this spirit, Collins books are packed with inspiration, innovation and practical expertise. They place you at the centre of a world of possibility and give you exactly what you need to explore it.

Collins. Freedom to teach.

Published by Collins
An imprint of HarperCollins*Publishers* Ltd.
77–85 Fulham Palace Road
Hammersmith
London
W6 8JB

**Browse the complete Collins catalogue at
www.collinseducation.com**

Previously published as *Collins Focus on Spelling*, first published 2002.

10 9 8 7 6 5 4 3

ISBN: 978-0-00-742658-4

Joyce Vallar and Carol Doncaster assert their moral right to be identified as the authors of this work.

British Library Cataloguing in Publication Data
A Catalogue record for this publication is available from the British Library.

Cover template: Laing and Carroll
Cover illustration: Q2A Media
Series design: Neil Adams and Garry Lambert
Illustrations: Shirley Chiang, Kevin Hopgood, Kerry Ingham, Claire Mumford, Andy Robb, Ross Thomson, Sarah Wimperis

Acknowledgement
The poem by T.W. Watt first appeared in the *Manchester Guardian*, 21 June 1954.

Every effort has been made to trace copyright holders and to obtain their permission for the use of copyright material. The authors and publisher will gladly receive any information enabling them to rectify any error or omission in subsequent editions.

Printed and bound by Printing Express Limited, Hong Kong.

Contents

Unit		Page
1	Adding *-s* and *-es* to make plurals	4
2	Other plurals	6
3	Plurals of nouns ending in vowels	8
4	The prefixes *auto-*, *bi-*, *over-*, *sub-*, *tele-* and *trans-*	10
5	The prefixes *fore-*, *kilo-*, *inter-*, and *mini-*	12
6	Word families	14
7	The suffixes *-ful* and *-fully*	16
Progress Unit 1		18
8	The suffix *-ing*	20
9	Soft *c*	22
10	Soft *g*	24
11	The letter strings *ear*, *ight* and *ough*	26
Progress Unit 2		28
12	Homophones	30
13	Possessive pronouns	32
14	The suffixes *-cian*, *-tion*, *-ssion*, and *-sion*	34
15	Syllables	36
16	Common suffixes	38
17	Using *ie* and *ei* (1)	40
18	Using *ie* and *ei* (2)	42
19	The prefixes *il-*, *im-*, *ir-*, and *in-*	44
Progress Unit 3		46
Spellchecker		48

Unit 1 Adding -s and -es to make plurals

How do you spell the plural of a noun that ends in a consonant, like *pen*?

For most nouns, add **-s**.

pen ⟶ pens

For nouns ending in **-ch**, **-s**, **-sh** or **-x**, add **-es**.

lunch ⟶ lunches

For nouns ending in a consonant + **y**, change **y** to **i** and add **-es**.

baby ⟶ babies

Getting started

1. **Copy this table.**
   Write the plural of each noun from the box in the correct column.

Add -s	Add -es
buttons	churches

button	church	meal	fax
patch	kiss	school	sister
batch	dish	balloon	

2. **Add three more nouns of your own to each column.**

More to think about

Change the underlined nouns into the plural.
Write the new sentences.

1. The <u>cook</u> in the <u>kitchen</u> cooked the <u>dish</u>.

2. The <u>class</u> welcomed the <u>visitor</u>.

3. The <u>fox</u> ran behind the thick <u>bush</u>.

4. The <u>boy</u> and <u>girl</u> waited for the <u>bus</u>.

5. The <u>bird</u> sat on the <u>branch</u> of the <u>oak</u>.

6. The <u>address</u> can be found in the <u>book</u>.

7. The <u>radish</u> and <u>pepper</u> added
   flavour to the <u>salad</u>.

Now try these

1. Write the plural of each noun.

   a) party → **parties**

   b) hobby

   c) baby

   d) library

   e) copy

   f) berry

   g) story

   h) pastry

   i) nappy

   j) lady

   k) curry

   l) battery

2. **Choose a pair of nouns (one singular and one plural) and use each word in a different sentence.**

Other plurals

How do you spell the plural of a noun that ends in *-f* or *-fe*, like *elf* or *wife*?

For most words that end in *-f*, change the **f** to **v** and add *-es*.

elf ⟶ elves

For most words that end in *-fe*, drop the **fe** and add *-ves*.

wife ⟶ wives

Some nouns have unusual plurals and need to be learned by heart.

ox ⟶ oxen
mouse ⟶ mice
goose ⟶ geese

Getting started

1. **Write the plural of each word.**
   The first one has been done to help you.

   a) scarf ➔ scarves   b) self   c) thief   d) half

   e) wolf   f) knife   g) loaf   h) life   i) calf

2. **This word does not end in *-f* or *-fe* in the singular.**

_____   _____

Write the word in the singular and the plural.

More to think about

Copy this table.
Write the plural of each noun in the correct column.

| loaf | roof | wife | half | leaf | reef | chief | hoof | thief |

Nouns that follow the rule	Nouns that do not follow the rule
loaves	roofs

Now try these

Some nouns have unusual plurals.

1. Copy the table.
   Write the singular and plural nouns from the box in the correct columns.

| goose | men | mouse | foot | child | teeth | woman | dice |

Singular	Plural
goose	

2. Now write the other form (singular or plural) of each noun in the table.

Plurals of nouns ending in vowels

How do you spell the plural of a noun that ends in a vowel, like *sofa* or *tomato*?

For most nouns ending in vowels, add **-s** to make the plural.

sofa + s ➡ sofas

For some nouns ending in **-o**, add **-es** to make the plural.

tomato ➡ tomatoes

Getting started

Write a plural noun to name each picture.

1.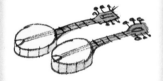

   banjos

2.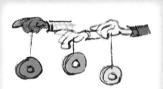

   _____

3.

   _____

4.

   _____

5.

   _____

6.

   _____

7.

   _____

8.

   _____

9.

   _____

More to think about

To make the plural of some nouns ending in **-o**, add **-es**.

Work out the clues, then write the answers and their plurals.

1. a person who has done something brave or good

   h_ero_ → _heroes_

2. a wild animal like a large cow, with long curved horns

   b_____ → _____

3. a white vegetable that has a brown or red skin and grows underground

   p_____ → _____

4. a mountain with an opening at the top from which lava sometimes erupts

   v_____ → _____

5. the repeat of a sound caused by the sound bouncing back off a surface

   e_____ → _____

6. a small, round, red fruit used as a vegetable

   t_____ → _____

7. a violent storm with strong circular winds around a funnel-shaped cloud

   t_____ → _____

Now try these

Add -s or -es to make each word plural. Use a dictionary to check the spellings.

1. cello → *cellos*

2. torpedo

3. disco

4. piano

5. cargo

6. logo

7. solo

8. flamingo

9. euro

The prefixes *auto-*, *bi-*, *over-*, *sub-*, *tele-* and *trans-*

What is a prefix? What does it do?
Let's look at the prefixes *auto-*, *bi-*, *over-*, *sub-*, *tele-* and *trans-*.

A prefix is a group of letters added to the beginning of a word.
A prefix can help you to work out the meaning of a word.

auto-	means "self"
bi-	means "two" or "twice"
over-	means "too much"
sub-	means "under" or "below"
tele-	means "distant"
trans-	means "across"

A *bi*cycle has <u>two</u> wheels.

An *over*loaded truck has <u>too big</u> a load.

Getting started

Add a prefix from the box to make a new word.
You can use each prefix more than once.

auto-	bi-	tele-	trans-	sub-	over-

1. phone → telephone
2. vision
3. focal
4. port
5. way
6. atlantic
7. scope
8. graph
9. plant
10. crowd
11. fill
12. focus

More to think about

1. **Write a definition for each of these words.**
   Use a dictionary to help you.

   a) overweight
   b) overflow
   c) bilingual
   d) bisect
   e) teletext
   f) telecommunications
   g) translate
   h) transfer

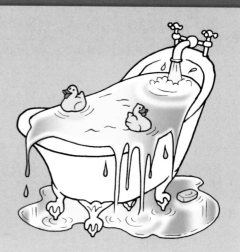

2. **Now choose four words from Question 1.**
   Use each word in a sentence.

Now try these

Use the clues to work out the words.
Each word starts with a different prefix from the box.
Use a dictionary to check the spellings.
The first one has been done to help you.

auto-	bi-	tele-	trans-
	sub-	over-	

1. An account of someone's life that they have written themselves.
   autobiography

2. A person who uses two languages is ...

3. A place thickly covered with plants and weeds is ...

4. A type of ship that can travel beneath the surface of the sea.

5. An operation where an organ is taken from one person and put into another.

6. When you become 100 years old you receive one of these from the Queen.

Unit 5

The prefixes *fore-*, *kilo-*, *inter-* and *mini-*

Let's look at the prefixes **fore-**, **kilo-**, **inter-** and **mini-**.

fore- means "before" or "at or near the front"

kilo- means "a thousand"

inter- means "between"

mini- means "smaller" or "less important"

Getting started

1. **Add a prefix from the box to make a new word.**
   You can use each prefix more than once.

fore-	kilo-	inter-	mini-

   a) cast → forecast

   b) gram

   c) metre

   d) national

   e) bus

   f) view

   g) ground

   h) beast

   i) name

   j) head

2. ***Inter-* means "between".**
   Use this information to work out the meanings of these words.
   Use a dictionary to check your answers.

   a) interactive

   b) intercom

   c) intermediate

More to think about

1. **Write each word and underline the prefix. The first one has been done to help you. Then write a definition for each word, using your dictionary to help you.**

   a) internet → <u>inter</u>net

   b) foreground

   c) forehead

   d) intersect

   e) miniskirt

   f) kilometre

2. **Now choose three words from Question 1, each beginning with a different prefix. Use each word in a sentence.**

Now try these

1. **Write each word and underline the prefix each time.**

   a) triangle → <u>tri</u>angle

   b) tricycle

   c) tripod

2. **What does the prefix mean?**

3. **Now use each word in a sentence.**

4. **Write a definition for each of these words. Check the definition in your dictionary.**

   a) triplets

   b) triple

   c) trio

Word families

What is a word family? How can it help you to spell?

Many words in the English language are developed from other words.
They belong to the same family.

build ⟶ **builder** ⟶ **building**

Knowing which family a word belongs to can help you to spell it.

Getting started

The words in the box can be sorted into four word families.
Write the words in the correct columns.

package	passenger	relation	actor
activity	packet	action	packing
passable	passage	related	relative

relate	pass	pack	act
related			

More to think about

To observe means "to watch something carefully".

1. **These definitions are all for words which have developed from the word *observe*.**
   Use the clues to work out the words.

   a) someone who notices things that are not usually noticed is ...

   b) a room or building containing telescopes for studying the moon, planets and stars

   c) a person who watches rather than takes part

To direct someone somewhere means "to tell them how to get there".

2. **These definitions are all for words which have developed from the word *direct*.**
   Use the clues to work out the words.

   a) a person who decides how a film or play is made or performed

   b) a book that gives lists of information such as names, addresses and telephone numbers

   c) instructions that tell you how to get somewhere

Now try these

Find at least two words that belong to each word family.
Write them in the correct columns.

music	hair	sign
musician		

15

The suffixes -*ful* and -*fully*

What is a suffix? What does it do?
Let's look at the suffixes **-ful** and **-fully**.

A suffix is a group of letters added at the end of a word.

For most words, just add **-ful** or **-fully**.

tear ⟶ tearful ⟶ tearfully

For words ending in a consonant + **y**,
change the **y** to **i** then add **-ful** or **-fully**.

beauty ⟶ beautiful ⟶ beautifully

Getting started

Copy and complete this table.

Word	Add -*ful*	Add -*fully*
play	playful	playfully
peace		
pity		
wonder		
fear		
mourn		
duty		
delight		
plenty		
power		
cheer		
faith		
truth		

More to think about

Choose a word from the box to complete each phrase.

> disgraceful   dutiful   powerful   tearful

1.

a _____ mess

2.

a _____ farewell

3.

a _____ machine

4.

a _____ daughter

Now try these

Add *-ful* or *-fully* to the root word to complete each sentence.

1. It is _doubtful_ that the match will take place.

doubt

2. Letters can be signed "Yours _____".

faith

3. The _____ puppy chewed the slippers.

play

4. The nurse _____ removed the glass from the wound.

care

5. Mr James is becoming very _____.

forget

Progress Unit 1

A. Write a plural noun to name each picture.

1.

d_____

2.

r_____

3.

t_____

4.

s_____

5.

w_____

6.

b_____

B. Add a prefix to complete each word.

1.

_____cycle

2.

_____graph

3.

_____phone

4.

_____port

5.

_____marine

6.

_____flow

C. Copy this table. Circle the words that belong to the same word family.

vary	varnish	(variety)	(various)
secret	secrecy	secretive	secure
miser	mischief	miserable	misery
occupy	occupation	occasion	occupant
hero	heroic	heroine	heron
music	musical	musician	museum

D. Choose words from the box to complete the sentences.

> doubtful   harmful   peaceful   awful   wrongful   dreadful

1. It is _____ if they will come again after the _____ journey.

2. A _____ arrest was made at the _____ demonstration.

3. The _____ substance had an _____ smell.

What happens when you add the suffix *-ing* to a word?

When a word has a short vowel sound and one consonant, *double* the last consonant before adding *-ing*.

rub ➡ rubbing

When a word has a long vowel sound, *do not double* the last consonant.

rain ➡ raining

When a word has two consonants after a short vowel sound, *do not double* the last consonant.

send ➡ sending

When a word ends in *-e*, drop the *e* before adding *-ing*.

hide ➡ hiding

Getting started

1. **Copy this table.**
   Write each word from the box in the correct column.

Long vowel	Short vowel
dream	snap

| dream | creep | snap | flit |
| swim | train | jog | break |

2. **Now add *-ing* to each word in your table.**

More to think about

1. **These words all have a short vowel sound.
   Add -ing to each word.**

   a) wrap → **wrapping**   b) lift

   c) bend   d) clap

   e) hit   f) rust

   g) chop   h) win

   i) slip   j) dust

   k) chat   l) melt

2. **Now sort your -ing words from Question 1
   into two types by completing this table.
   Write a heading for each column.**

wrapping	lifting

3. **These words all end in -e.
   Add -ing to each word.**

   a) ride   b) slope   c) write   d) blame   e) tune

Now try these

The *-ing* words in these sentences have been spelled wrongly.
Write the sentences correctly.
The first one has been done to help you.

1. The joiner is fiting a new lock on the window.

   The joiner is fitting a new lock on the window.

2. We went skatting on the frozen pond.

3. I am hopping to win the hoping race.

4. The man is moping the sticky floor.

5. The dog was chaseing the cat.

Soft *c*

How do you spell words with the soft *c* sound, like *century*?

The letter **c** makes the sound "**s**" when it is followed by **e**, **i** or **y**.

cymbals

decide

century

Getting started

1. **Circle the soft *c* sound in each word. The first one has been done to help you.**

    a) bi(c)ycle

    b) accident

    c) chance

    d) concert

    e) practice

    f) certificate

    g) circle

    h) circular

    i) circus

    j) success

    k) circumference

    l) concern

2. **Now choose three words from Question 1 and use each word in a sentence.**

More to think about

A soft *c* has been missed out of these words.
Write the words correctly, putting the letter *c* in the correct place.
Circle the *c* in each word.
Two have been done to help you.

1. elery ➡ ©elery
2. stenil ➡ sten©il
3. ymbals
4. deimal
5. exept
6. inema
7. reent
8. entury
9. groer
10. ell
11. deide
12. ity
13. ereal
14. Deember

Now try these

New words can be made from one word by changing the **onset** (the first sound).

In the word **price**, **pr** is the onset.

pr   +   ice   =   price
onset

1. **Change the onset to make new words.**
   Write at least four new rhyming words in each box.

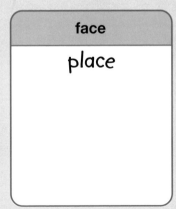

face

place

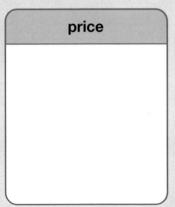

price

2. **Now use one set of rhyming words to write a short poem.**

How do you spell words with the soft **g** sound, like *magic*?

A soft **g** sounds like **j** as in *jar*.

A soft **g** is usually spelled with a **g** before **e**, **i** or **y**.

germ

A soft **g** sound is usually spelled with a **g** when it comes in the middle of a word.

magic

A soft **g** sound is usually spelled **-ge** when it comes at the end of a word.

cage

Getting started

Copy and complete this table using the words in the box.

Soft *g*	Hard *g*
giant	garden

giant   garden   giraffe   gentle
goose   gym   garlic   golf   general
ginger   gobble   genius   goldfish
gallop   gardener   gerbil

More to think about

1. **Write a word to name each picture.**

_____ _____ _____

2. **Use the clues to work out the words.**

   a) someone you have never met before
      str_____

   b) an event or situation that is disastrous or very sad
      tr_____

   c) a bird with grey feathers, often seen in towns
      p_____

   d) a moveable joint that attaches a door or window to its frame
      h_____

   e) a boat with a flat bottom, used for carrying heavy loads
      b_____

Now try these

Rhyming can help you to spell.
Write four rhyming words in each box.

cage	nudge
rage	

The letter strings *ear*, *ight* and *ough*

Did you know that the same letters can make different sounds?
Let's look at the letter strings **ear**, **ight** and **ough**.

The letter string **ear** can have different pronunciations.

ear as in beard

air as in pear

er   as in earth

ar   as in heart

The letter string **ight** can sound like **ite**.

ni*ght*

When the letter **e** comes before **ight**, the letter string can sound like **ate**.

we*ight*

Getting started

1. **Add the letter string *ear* to complete these words.**

    a) d**ear**   b) b_____

    c) s_____ch   d) cl_____

    e) _____n   f) n_____

    g) l_____n   h) f_____

    i) sp_____   j) g_____

    k) w_____   l) h_____d

2. **Copy and complete this table using the words from Question 1.**

Sounds like *pear*	Sounds like *beard*	Sounds like *earth*
	dear	

More to think about

1. Add *ight* or *eight* to complete these words.

a) r**ight**   b) w**eight**

c) f_____   d) br_____

e) fr_____   f) l_____

2. Copy and complete this table using the words from Question 1.

Sounds like *kite*	Sounds like *ate*

Now try these

The letter string **ough** can represent different sounds.

I take it you already know
of tough and bough and cough and dough?
Others may stumble but not you,
On hiccough, thorough, laugh and through.
Well done! And now you wish, perhaps,
To learn of more familiar traps.

Extract from a letter published in the London Times
(3 January 1965)

1. Write the words in the poem that have the same letter string.
   How many different pronunciations are there?

2. These *ough* words sound like four *ough* words in the poem.
   Match each word with a word it sounds like from the poem.

   trough   rough   though   borough

Progress Unit 2

A. Write a word to name each picture. Each word contains a soft *c* sound.

1.

_____

2.
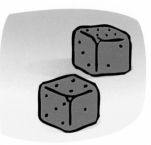
_____

3.
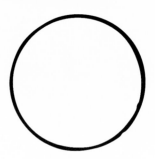
_____

4.

_____

5.

_____

6.

_____

B. Write a word to name each picture. Each word contains a soft *g* sound.

1.

_____

2.

_____

3.

_____

4.

_____

5.
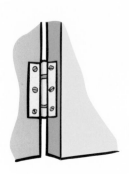
_____

6.

_____

C. Write a word to name each picture.

1.

h_____

2.

d_____

3.

b_____

4.

r_____

5.

fr_____

6.

c_____

D. Choose the correct word to name each picture.

1.

pale, pail

2.

chute, shoot

3.

seller, cellar

4.

flour, flower

5.

heel, heal

6.

break, brake

Homophones

Did you know that some words sound the same but have different spellings, like **by** and **buy**?

Words that sound the same but have different spellings are called homophones.

Nusrin waved good*bye* as she went *by* bus to *buy* some shoes.

Getting started

Write a definition for each word.
Use a dictionary to help you.

Word	Definition
waste	rubbish that is no longer wanted
waist	the middle part of your body where it narrows slightly above your hips
grate	
great	
sell	
cell	
hole	
whole	

More to think about

1. **Choose the correct homophone from the box to complete each sentence.**

peace	bored	plane	piece	plain	board

a) Here is a large _____ of cake.

b) At last, there was _____ and quiet.

c) The wheel on the skate_____ was broken.

d) Darren was _____ by the wedding speeches.

e) The pastry chef used _____ flour.

f) The _____ made an emergency landing.

2. **There are four more words in the sentences in Question 1 which have homophones. The words begin with *h*, *t*, *f* and *m*. Write the words and their homophones. The first one has been done to help you.**

here + hear

Now try these

Find two homophones for each word.
The first one has been done to help you.

by	buy	bye
to		
so		
rain		
road		
sent		

Possessive pronouns

What are possessive pronouns? How are they used?

Possessive pronouns can be used instead of people's names.
They tell us who things belong to.

This is Mary's coat.

The coat is *hers*.

That is the Smiths' house.

The house is *theirs*.

Getting started

Use a possessive pronoun from the box to complete each sentence.
You can only use each pronoun once.

| ours | hers | his | theirs | mine |

1.
The book is <u>hers</u>.

2. The bikes are _____.

3. The shoe is _____.

4. The helmet is _____.

5. The computer is _____.

More to think about

1. **Complete each sentence with a possessive pronoun.**

   a) This is Nicole's hat. This hat is _____.

   b) This is Abdul's bike. This bike is _____.

   c) This is Gavin's book. This book is _____.

   d) That is Mr and Mrs Thomson's car.
   That car is _____.

2. **Choose the correct word to complete each sentence.**
   Underline the possessive pronouns you have used.

   a) That is my parcel.
   That parcel is_____. (mine, theirs)

   b) That is your book.
   The book is _____. (ours, yours)

   c) Those are Lola's sweets.
   Those sweets are _____. (mine, hers)

   d) That is our classroom.
   The classroom is_____. (ours, his)

   e) Those are Bill's, Ted's and Adi's toys.
   The toys are _____. (his, theirs)

Now try these

Change the underlined words to possessive pronouns.
The first one has been done to help you.

1. The car is <u>Jenny's</u>. → hers

2. The car is <u>Jack's</u>.

3. The car is <u>Mr and Mrs Patek's</u>.

The suffixes *-cian*, *-tion*, *-ssion* and *-sion*

How do you spell words that end with **-cian**, **-tion**, **-ssion** or **-sion**?

The suffixes **-cian**, **-tion** and **-ssion** can make the sound **shun** at the end of words. The suffix **-sion** can make the sound **zjun**.

The suffix **-tion** is the most common ending.

fiction

The suffix **-cian** is often used for jobs.

musician

The suffix **-sion** is used when the root word ends in **-de** or **-se**.

explode ⟶ explosion

confuse ⟶ confusion

Getting started

1. Add *-cian* to complete these jobs.

a) politi**cian** b) beauti_____ c) techni_____

2. Write a job to name each picture.

a)

o_____

b)

e_____

c)

m_____

More to think about

Choose the correct suffix from the box to complete each word.
Use the clues to help you work out the words.

| -ation | -ition | -otion | -ution |

1. a liquid that you put on your skin to
   protect or soften it → l**otion**

2. learning and teaching → educ_____

3. something that happens again → repet_____

4. any substance that contaminates air,
   water or land → poll_____

5. the layer of concrete on which a building
   is constructed → found_____

6. an event to find who is best at something → compet_____

7. movement → m_____

8. a complete turn of 360° → revol_____

Now try these

Copy this newspaper report, choosing the correct spelling to fill each gap.

There was much panic and **confusion** (confusion), **confussion**) today
after a _____ (**collission**, **collision**) between a tanker and a lorry.

An _____ (**explosion**, **explossion**) was heard shortly after the crash.
Many people were injured and the driver of the tanker was given
a blood _____ (**transfusion**, **transfussion**) at the scene of the accident.
When the police are in _____ (**possesion**, **possession**) of all the facts
a _____ (**discusion**, **discussion**) will take place.

35

Syllables

How can dividing a word into syllables help with spelling?

Most words can be divided into syllables.
Some syllables have vowels that are hard to hear.
These are called unstressed vowels.

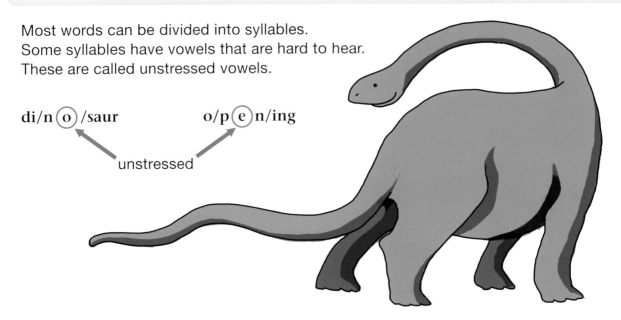

di/n(o)/saur   o/p(e)n/ing

unstressed

Pronouncing each syllable slowly and in an exaggerated way can help with spelling.

Getting started

Divide these words into syllables and complete the table.

Word	Syllables	Number of syllables
computer	com/pu/ter	3
desperate		
separate		
hospital		
forgotten		
adventure		
difficult		
roundabout		
general		

More to think about

In the word *demonstrate* the syllables are dem/on/strate.
When you say the word aloud, the unstressed vowel is **o**.

Write a three-syllable word to name each picture.
Circle the unstressed vowel in each word.

1.

din(o)saur

2.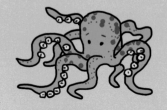

o_____

3.

e_____

4.

b_____

5.

f_____

6.

a_____

7.

a_____

8.

m_____

9.

e_____

Now try these

Add suffixes to turn these two-syllable words into three-syllable words.
The first one has been done to help you.

1. visit**or**
2. equip____
3. comfort____
4. forget____
5. open____
6. power____
7. subtract____
8. record____
9. owner____
10. willing____
11. employ____
12. neighbour____

Common suffixes

What happens when you add suffixes like **-ed** or **-less** to a word?

If the word ends in **-e**, drop the **e** before adding a vowel suffix such as **-ed** or **-ing**.

hope ⟶ hoped ⟶ hoping

Keep the **e** when adding a consonant suffix such as **-less**.

care ⟶ careless

If the word ends in **-y**, change the **y** to **i** when adding a suffix such as **-ness**.

happy ⟶ happiness

But do not change the **y** to **i** when adding **-ing**.

play ⟶ playing

hurry ⟶ hurrying

Getting started

1. Add the suffix to the root word.

a) live + ed = lived

b) shame + less   c) pretty + er

d) carry + ing   e) windy + est

f) tune + ing   g) use + ful

h) spite + ful   i) supply + ing

2. Write the root word and the suffix.

a) skating = skate + ing

b) later   c) exciting

d) cheekiest   e) tireless

f) copied   g) beautiful

More to think about

Use all the suffixes to make new words.

1. **tune**
   - -ing → *tuning*
   - -ed → *tuned*
   - -ful
   - -less

2. **use**
   - -ing
   - -ed
   - -ful
   - -less

3. **care**
   - -ing
   - -ed
   - -ful
   - -less

4. **pity**
   - -ing
   - -ed
   - -ful
   - -less

5. **empty**
   - -ing
   - -ed
   - -er
   - -est
   - -ness

Now try these

Some words in these signs have been spelled wrongly.
Write the signs correctly.

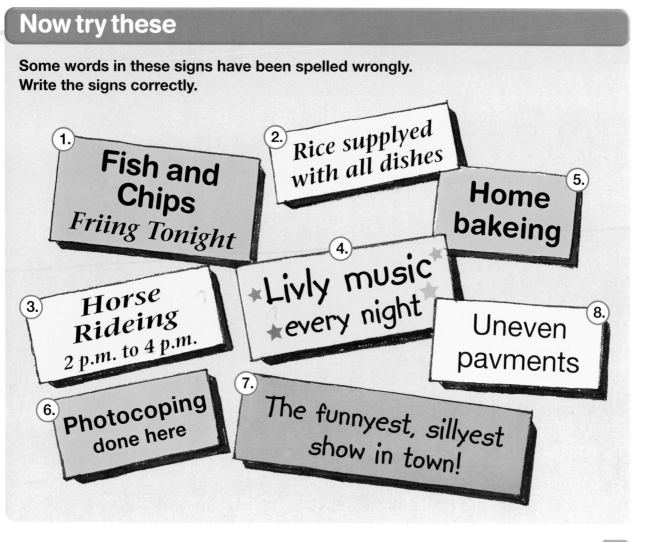

1. Fish and Chips *Friing Tonight*

2. Rice supplyed with all dishes

3. Horse Rideing 2 p.m. to 4 p.m.

4. ★Livly music★ every night

5. Home bakeing

6. Photocoping done here

7. The funnyest, sillyest show in town!

8. Uneven pavments

Using *ie* and *ei* (1)

How do you know whether to spell a word with **ie** or **ei**, like *piece* or *receive*?

In most words **i** comes before **e**.

piece

But after **c**, **e** comes before **i**.

receive

So remember: **i** before **e** except after **c**.

Getting started

1. **The letters *ie* can make a long *i* sound, as in *tie*.**
    Write three words that rhyme with *tie*.

    a) ____ie   b) ____ie   c) ____ie

2. **The letters *ie* can also make a long *e* sound, as in *piece*.**
    Write a word to name each picture.

    a)    b)    c)

3. **The letters *ier* can sound like *ear*, as in *tier*.**
    Write a word to name each picture.

    a)    b)    c)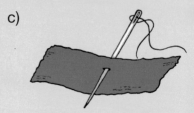

    p_____   f_____ce   p_____ce

More to think about

Copy and complete this table using the words in the box.

Long e sound	Long i sound	Sounds like ear
piece	pie	pierce

piece	pierce	pie	field
niece	tier	brief	cried
pier	tried	tie	lie
dried	fierce	priest	thief

Now try these

Complete these words with *ie* or *ei*.
Use your dictionary to check the spellings.

1. shr ie k
2. f___ld
3. n___ce
4. rec___ve
5. conc___ted
6. dec___t
7. rec___pt
8. rel___f
9. bel___ve
10. c___ling
11. gr___f
12. conc___t

How do you know whether to spell a word with **ie** or **ei**, like *chief*, *receive* or *weigh*?

In most words **i** comes before **e**, except after **c**.

chief   receive

However, sometimes **ei** can sound like **ai**.

Use **ei** when **ei** sounds like **ai**.

weigh

Use **ei** after **c** when **ei** sounds like **ee**.

ceiling

Getting started

Sort the words from the box into two columns.

ei sounds like ee	ei sounds like ai
receipt	sleigh

sleigh   vein   freight   receipt
reign   veil   neighbour   deceive
perceive   weight   rein   deceit
receive   conceit   conceive

More to think about

1. Write these numbers in words.

   a) 8   b) $80\frac{1}{8}$ c) 88   d) 18

2. Write a homophone that contains the letters *ei* for each word.

   a) rain

   b) way

   c) slay

   d) wait

   e) vain

   f) there

3. Choose two pairs of homophones from Question 2.
   Write a sentence using each word.

Now try these

1. Add *-ceive* to each prefix to make a word.
   The first one has been done to help you.

   | de- | re- | con- | per- | + ceive |

   de + ceive = deceive

2. Check the meaning of each word in your dictionary and write a definition.

3. Use each word in a sentence.

Unit 19 The prefixes *il-*, *im-*, *ir-* and *in-*

Let's look at the prefixes *il-*, *im-*, *ir-* and *in-*.

The prefixes *il-*, *im-*, *ir-* and *in-* all mean "not".

The prefix *il-* is usually added to words beginning with *l*.

*il*legal

The prefix *im-* is usually added to words beginning with *m* and *p*.

*im*mobile   *im*patient

The prefix *ir-* is usually added to words beginning with *r*.

*ir*regular

The prefix *in-* is added to most other words.

*in*definite

Getting started

Add the prefix *im-* to these words to make their antonyms (opposites). Use a dictionary to check the meaning of each word.

1. mature →    2. migrate

3. mobile   4. moral

5. mortal   6. patient

7. perfect   8. possible

9. practical   10. probable

11. moveable   12. partial

More to think about

1. **Add the prefix *in-* to these words.**

   a) complete → **incomplete**   b) accurate   c) audible

   d) adequate   e) capable   f) considerable

   g) flammable   h) formal   i) secure

   j) significant   k) human   l) justice

2. **Choose three pairs of words from Question 1.**
   Use each pair in one sentence.

Now try these

Add *ir-* or *il-* to these words to make new words.

1. legible → **illegible**   2. regular   3. legal

4. rational   5. logical   6. reversible

7. literate   8. responsible   9. relevant

Progress Unit 3

A. Write a word to name each picture. They all end in *-ion*.

1.

   i_____

2.

   f_____

3.

   p_____

4.

   d_____

5.

   l_____

6.

   c_____

B. Divide these words into syllables and complete the table. Circle the unstressed vowel in each word.

Word	Syllables
motorist	
desperate	
factory	
deafening	
interest	
definite	

C. Write a word to name each picture.

1.

_____

2.

_____

3.

_____

4.

_____

5.

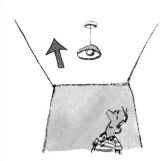

_____

6.

_____

D. Add the correct prefix from the box to make a new word.

| im- | ir- | in- | il- |

1. ___resistible

2. ___literate

3. ___perfect

4. ___convenient

5. ___correct

6. ___regular

7. ___practical

8. ___legal

9. ___polite

✓ Spellchecker

Write these signs correctly. Then check the spellings in your dictionary.

1. **Bisycle lane**

2. **Sinema Tikkets**

3. Optision
······
Grate offer!
······
By won pear, get another pear **free!**

4. Breakfast Serial

75p

5. Wieght training at your local jym

6. Lunchs served daily

Baked potatos
Pizzaes
Fruit salad
- mangos
- pairs
- pineapples
Filled rolles